Cupcakes & Cookies

First published in Great Britain 2011

Search Press Limited
Wellwood, North Farm Road,
Tunbridge Wells, Kent TN2 3DR
Text copyright © Frances McNaughton, Lisa Slatter 2011

Based on the following books published by Search Press:
Twenty to Make: Decorated Cupcakes by Frances McNaughton (2009)
Twenty to Make: Decorated Cookies by Lisa Slatter (2010)

Photographs by Roddy Paine Photographic Studio (pages 1, 5–49 and 96) and
Debbie Patterson at Search Press Studios (pages 2–4 and 50–95)

Photographs and design copyright © Search Press Ltd 2011

ISBN: 978-1-84448-663-2

Suppliers
If you have difficulty in obtaining any of the materials and equipment
mentioned in this book, then please visit the Search Press website for details
of suppliers: www.searchpress.com

A note on sugar:

The US equivalent of caster sugar is
superfine sugar, and the equivalent of
icing sugar is confectioner's sugar.

Printed in China

Cupcakes & Cookies

Decorations for all Occasions

Frances McNaughton
and Lisa Slatter

Search Press

Contents

Decorated Cookies 50

Decorated Cupcakes

by Frances McNaughton

Small is the new big! Cupcakes are a very popular way of celebrating any special occasion. They can be a colourful and tasty display for any party table. Some modern weddings even choose cupcakes as the centrepiece. Even if you don't have a special occasion, why not just make cakes for family and friends – it's a great way of practising recipes and icing ideas to use on larger cakes.

There are many different cake recipes which can be used to make delicious cupcakes – in fact most cake recipes for large cakes are also suitable for making small cakes.

More and more people are discovering the delights of cake decorating by having a go at making cupcakes. I hope you have fun trying some of my ideas, and that having a go will spark a few ideas of your own.

Just some of the mouthwatering cupcakes that you can make using the techniques shown in this chapter.

Making cupcakes

This all-in-one sponge cake recipe makes twelve small cupcakes:

115g (4oz) self-raising flour, sieved
115g (4oz) soft cake margarine or soft butter
115g (4oz) caster sugar
2 eggs

1 Preheat the oven to 180°C/350°F/Gas mark 4. Line a cupcake tin with paper cases. Different tin sizes are available, and you can buy paper cases to go with each size.

2 Put all the ingredients in a bowl.

3 Beat with a wooden spoon for 2–3 minutes. If using a food mixer, reduce the beating time: only beat until the mixture becomes smooth and glossy.

4 Spoon the mixture into the cases – about half full for flatter cakes, about three-quarters full for more domed cakes.

5 Bake in the centre of the oven for 15–20 minutes until golden and the tops spring back when pressed gently. Allow a longer baking time for deeper and larger cakes.

A large range of flat-iced cupcakes, plain fairy cakes and muffins are available in supermarkets and bakeries for those who just want to do the icing part! Small jelly sweets, melted chocolate, chocolate-covered stick biscuits, soft, golden sugar, edible glitter flakes and soft fudge have been used in this book to create simple designs.

Alternative flavours

Chocolate: add 15ml/1 tablespoon of cocoa powder mixed with 15ml/1 tablespoon of boiling water.

Lemon: add 10ml/2 teaspoons of lemon juice and 5 ml/1 teaspoon of grated lemon rind.

Coffee: add 10ml/2 teaspoons of instant coffee dissolved in 5ml/1 teaspoon of hot water.

You can make different sizes from small sweet cases through to large muffin cases. Depending on the design you want to make, the cake can be baked so that it only fills up to the top of the case when baked, for a flat design; or it can be baked with more cake in the case, to form a dome when it is baked. If the cake rises more than you want, or is cracked on the surface, simply carve off the top to make it domed or flat.

Basic tools

Piping bags with piping tubes/nozzles

Small cutters in shapes such as primrose, small rose petal, holly leaf and heart

Round biscuit cutters (plain and frilly)

Quilt embosser

Cutting wheel

Flower centre tool

Small palette knife

Small rolling pin

Small, sharp scissors

Over the Rainbow

Materials:

Cupcakes in brightly coloured cases

White frosting:

    170g (6oz) white vegetable fat (shortening)

    450g (16oz) icing sugar

    3–4 tablespoons (45–60ml) milk or lemon juice

    Vanilla essence

Food colourings: blue, red, yellow and green

Tools:

Small palette knife

At least four greaseproof paper piping bags

No. 3 or 4 plain piping tube (or snip the end off a paper piping bag)

Instructions:

1 Make the white frosting by mixing the fat, sugar and flavouring, then beat in a few drops of lemon juice or milk to form a smooth, soft icing for piping. Using white vegetable fat keeps the icing white for the clouds, and blue for the sky. If you prefer to use butter for a better flavour, the clouds will look creamy and the blue will not be so bright.

2 Mix a portion of the frosting with red food colouring, another with yellow and another with green. Fill the piping bags (with or without the piping tubes) with a large spoonful each of frosting: white, red, yellow and green.

3 Mix blue colouring into the rest of the frosting and spread over the surface of each cake with a palette knife.

4 Pipe a curved red line half way round each cake, then repeat with the yellow, then the green.

5 Pipe little clouds at the ends of the rainbow.

Colourful rainbow cupcakes like these will brighten any party table.

Halloween Pumpkin

Materials:

Cupcakes baked in brightly coloured cases

Buttercream:

    150g (6oz) butter

    450g (16oz) icing sugar

    3–4 tablespoons (45–60ml) milk or lemon juice

Food colourings: egg yellow or orange; green

Dark chocolate, melted

Tools:

Small palette knife

Greaseproof paper piping bags

No. 2 plain piping tube

No. 4 plain piping tube (or snip the end
    off a paper piping bag)

Non-stick baking paper

Instructions:

1 Make the buttercream by mixing the butter and sugar,
then beating in a few drops of milk or lemon juice to
form a smooth, soft icing for piping.

2 Mix green colouring into a small portion of
the buttercream and orange into the rest.
Fill a small piping bag fitted with a No. 2
plain piping tube with a small spoonful of
green buttercream. Fill a larger piping
bag fitted with a No. 4 plain piping tube
with orange-coloured buttercream.

3 Start the piping with a straight
orange line down the centre, and then
pipe either side, increasing the curve
as each line is piped.

4 Pipe a few green lines at the top
for leaves.

5 Put a small amount of melted dark
chocolate into a small piping bag, and
snip off a tiny piece of the end. You can
then pipe a face directly on the cake.
Alternatively, pipe it on to non-stick baking
paper and leave it to set, then peel it off and
stick it to the cake.

Make as many different scary pumpkin faces as you like for a Halloween party, or to hand out to trick-or-treaters.

Life's a Beach

Materials:

Cupcakes baked in brightly coloured cases

Fondant icing mix (not sugarpaste), available from sugarcraft shops and some supermarkets

Pink sugarpaste or modelling sugarpaste

Food colourings: blue and pink

Soft, golden caster sugar

Tools:

Small palette knife

Use the picture (right) to trace around the flip-flops to make a card template

Sharp knife or cutting wheel

Small rolling pin

Bowl

The templates for the flip-flops.

Instructions:

1 Using pink sugarpaste or modelling sugarpaste and the flip-flop templates, roll out and cut out the soles of the flip-flops. Cut out thin straps, dampen them with water and stick them on.

2 Mix the fondant icing, following the instructions on the packet. Gently warm to body temperature in a bowl over hot water, stirring occasionally. The fondant will be quite runny, but sets quite quickly as it cools.

3 Colour half of the fondant blue, and leave the other half white.

4 Spread blue fondant on half of each cake, and white on the other half.

5 Sprinkle the white half with soft, golden caster sugar, to look like sand.

6 Lay the flip-flops on top of each cake. If you want to make sure they are stuck on, spread a small dot of warmed fondant or buttercream under each heel, to act as glue.

Lazy Summer

For a variation, add a few drops of liquid green colour to desiccated coconut or granulated sugar, to look like grass. Dip half of the cupcake in the 'grass' to stick it on. Perfect for a summer party.

Beautiful Basket

Materials:

Cupcakes

Fondant icing mix (see page 14)

Chocolate buttercream:

> see the recipe on page 12, and add up to 30ml/2 tablespoons cocoa powder until you get the shade you like

Yellow sugarpaste for primroses

Tools:

Small palette knife

Greaseproof paper piping bags

Piping tube: small basketweave, rope or star

Small primrose flower cutter

Flower centre tool

Small rolling pin

Instructions:

1 Spread the fondant icing on top of each cake. This can be coloured if you prefer.

2 Fill a piping bag fitted with a basketweave, rope, or star piping tube with chocolate buttercream.

3 Start by piping the handle on top of each cake.

4 Then pipe a basket: start at one side, piping a vertical line, then pipe short lines across it, leaving the width of the piping tube between each line. Pipe a second vertical line, just covering the ends of the short horizontal lines. Pipe short lines across this second line, filling the gaps between the first and second vertical lines. Pipe a third vertical line and continue piping short horizontal lines across. Continue across the cake until the basket is completed.

5 Roll out yellow sugarpaste and cut out primrose flowers. Stick on to the cupcake at the top of the basket by pushing the centre in with the flower centre tool.

Easter Egg Hunt

Make the basket in the same way, and add colourful jelly beans or tiny Easter eggs.

Fluffy Duck

Materials:

Cupcakes

Fondant icing (see page 14) coloured with blue food colouring

Buttercream (see page 12) coloured with yellow food colouring

Red or orange sugarpaste

Small amount of melted dark chocolate for the eye

Tools:

Small palette knife

Piping bags

Large, plain piping tube

Instructions:

1 Spread the warmed blue fondant on each cake.

2 Fit the piping bag with the large, plain piping tube and fill it with yellow buttercream.

3 Pipe a large ball for the head.

4 Pipe a large, fat curved teardrop for the body, starting at the front. Pipe a smaller teardrop for the wing, marking it with a palette knife for the feathers.

5 Make a small beak from orange or red sugarpaste and stick it into the soft buttercream.

6 Pipe an eye with melted dark chocolate in a piping bag.

Swanning Around

Make a swan in white frosting (see page 10 for recipe), starting with a long, curved head and neck. Pipe the dark beak and the eyes with chocolate.

Lionheart

Materials:

Cupcakes

Chocolate buttercream:

> See recipe on page 12, adding up to 30ml/2 tablespoons of cocoa powder until you get the shade you like

Sugarpaste coloured with autumn leaf colouring for the face. (Alternatively, use soft commercial fudge sweets. These can be warmed in the hands and moulded to shape)

Small amount of melted dark chocolate for the features

Tools:

Piping bags

Piping tube: basketweave, small rope or star

Small rolling pin

Heart cutter

Cocktail stick

Instructions:

1 Fill a piping bag fitted with a basketweave, rope, or star piping tube with chocolate buttercream.

2 Pipe wiggly lines starting at the centre and finishing with the point over the edge of the cake.

3 Mould coloured sugarpaste (or soft fudge) to form a heart shape. Use the picture as a guide, or roll out the paste and cut out using a heart-shaped cutter. Lay it on the cake.

4 Shape two small ovals for the cheeks. Press into place and mark with a cocktail stick.

5 Make two tiny balls of paste for the ears, flatten them slightly and pinch each base.

6 Pipe the eyes, nose and eyebrows with melted dark chocolate.

Tiger, Tiger

To make the tiger, use a plain piping tube and orange-coloured buttercream (see page 12) to pipe on to the cake. Shape the face in the same way as the lion using white sugarpaste. Pipe stripes, eyes, nose, and eyebrows with melted dark chocolate.

Checkmate

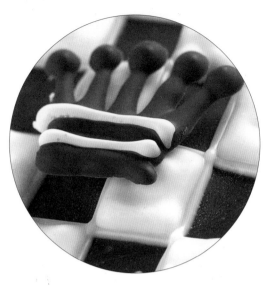

Materials:

Cupcakes with flat tops (cut the tops off if necessary)

225g (8oz) dark chocolate, melted

225g (8oz) white chocolate, melted

Tools:

Small palette knife

Piping bags

Non-stick baking paper

The templates for the chess pieces.

Instructions:

1 Fill a small piping bag with melted dark chocolate and another with melted white chocolate.

2 Using the templates as a guide, pipe out the chess pieces on to non-stick baking paper. Set aside somewhere cool, to harden.

3 Spread the top of each cake with dark chocolate.

4 Pipe thin, straight lines across each cake with white chocolate, then pipe the other way to form a grid of squares. Fill in alternate squares with the melted white chocolate.

5 When the chess pieces are set, remove carefully from the non-stick paper and stick to each cake with a dot of melted chocolate.

Dark Knight

Make a whole chess set and decorate each chess piece with chocolate in the opposite colour. If you prefer the taste of white chocolate, start each cake by spreading with white, instead of dark, chocolate. Perfect for the chess champion in your life.

Baby Blanket

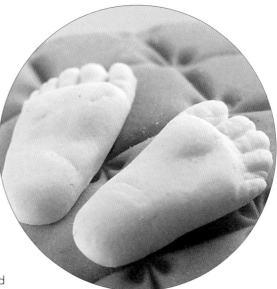

Materials:

Cupcakes

Sugarpaste in blue or pink and white

Icing sugar for rolling out sugarpaste

Small amount of jam or buttercream (see page 12), to stick the blanket to the cake

Tools:

Small rolling pin

Quilting embosser (or quilting can be marked on the sugarpaste using a knife with a ruler)

Tiny feet mould (alternatively, the feet can be modelled by hand from sugarpaste or piped using white frosting – recipe on page 10 – using the photograph as a guide)

Cutting wheel or knife

Square template made from card, slightly larger than the top of the cake

Opposite
Blue for a Boy
These delicate cupcakes are ideal for a baby shower or christening, or as a gift to celebrate a new arrival.

Instructions:

1 Roll out the sugarpaste in the colour of your choice, using icing sugar to stop it sticking to the work surface.

2 Emboss the surface of the icing to look like a quilted blanket.

3 Using your prepared template, cut the icing to form a square.

4 Spread a small amount of buttercream or jam on top of the cake and lay the icing blanket on top, with the points overhanging the edge.

5 Make tiny feet from white sugarpaste and stick on top of your cupcake.

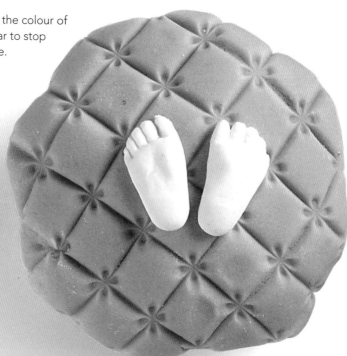

Knitted Novelties

Materials:

At least seven cupcakes (can be domed or flat)

White frosting (see page 10)

Food colouring: I used yellow, green and blue to match the cases, but choose your own colours

Candy sticks from sweet shops

Small amount of white sugarpaste for the ends of the knitting needles

Tools:

Piping bags

Plain piping tube No. 3 or No. 4

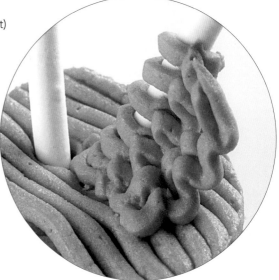

Instructions:

1 Mix your chosen colours into the white frosting and place each in a piping bag fitted with a plain piping tube.

2 Pipe straight lines across each cake as shown, to look like loosely rolled balls of wool.

3 Pipe a spiral line down one of the candy sticks and push the end of the stick into one of the cupcakes.

4 Continue piping loops in rows along the stick to look like knitting.

5 Push the other candy stick into the same cupcake.

6 Dampen the top ends of the candy sticks and press a small flattened ball of sugarpaste on to each one.

This colourful collection of cupcakes would be ideal for celebrating the birthday of a friend who loves knitting.

Daisy Daisy

Materials:

At least nine flat-topped cupcakes

White frosting (see page 10)

Food colouring: yellow for the flower centre and green for leaves

Tools:

Small palette knife

Piping bags

Large, plain piping tube

Instructions:

1 Mix yellow food colouring with some of the frosting and green with another portion, and leave the rest white. Spread the white frosting over the tops of six of the cakes.

2 Pipe large petals across each cake using a plain piping tube.

3 Pipe a large yellow swirl on top of one cake using a large, plain piping tube.

4 Spread green frosting over two of the cakes.

5 Pipe large green leaves (shown on the opposite page) using a plain or a leaf piping tube.

Celebrate a keen gardener, or a friend named Daisy, with this crazy daisy cupcake display.

Spanish Fan

Materials:

Cupcakes baked in red cases

Buttercream (see page 12 for recipe)

Red food colouring

Food colouring powders: red and
   edible gold

Edible painting solution/alcohol

Sugar modelling paste

Tools:

Small palette knife

Piping bags

Piping tube: star or rope

*The template
for the fan.*

Instructions:

1 Make fans by rolling out thin sugar
modelling paste using the template. Mark
lines on the fans with a palette knife.

2 Paint the fans with red powder food
colouring and edible gold powder,
each mixed with painting
solution/alcohol. Leave the fans
to dry, preferably overnight,
turning occasionally.

3 Spread the tops
of the cupcakes with
red buttercream.

4 Pipe around the edge
of each cake using a star
or rope tube.

5 Push the dry fans into the
tops of the cupcakes.

This fantastic cupcake has a Spanish look, but you could change the colours to create an oriental theme.

Strawberry Cream

Materials:

Cupcakes: as a variation, you could put a single strawberry in each case before you put the cake batter in – it will then cook inside the cake

White chocolate ganache: 1 part double cream to 3 parts white chocolate; e.g.

    150g (6oz) double cream

    450g (18oz) white chocolate

Fresh strawberries

Tools:

Piping bags

Piping tube: large star or rope

Instructions:

1 Melt the white chocolate. Bring the double cream to the boil and immediately turn off the heat. Mix together. Leave to cool in a fridge until thick enough to pipe with. If the ganache is too stiff, allow it to come back to room temperature, or beat it in a food mixer, adding a little more double cream to help soften it.

2 Pipe a large swirl of white chocolate ganache on top of each cupcake, starting from the outside edge and coming up to a point in the middle.

3 Decorate with a fresh strawberry.

Opposite
Raspberry Reverie
For a delicious dark chocolate alternative, use chocolate cake instead of vanilla, and put a raspberry in the bottom of the cake before it is cooked. Dark chocolate ganache is made with equal parts of chocolate to buttercream; e.g. 300g (12oz) double cream to 300g (12oz) dark chocolate.

Ice Cream Dream

Materials:

Flat-bottomed ice cream cones

Crispy rice breakfast cereal

100g (3½oz) white chocolate, melted

Buttercream (see page 12)

Ice cream sauce, fruit flavour

Tools:

Piping bag

Piping tube: large star or rope

Instructions:

1 Mix melted white chocolate with the crispy rice cereal – enough to coat each grain to make them stick together. Fill each of the ice cream cones to a dome on top (see above). Leave to cool.

2 Pipe a large swirl of buttercream, starting from the outside edge and coming up to a point in the middle.

3 Drizzle the top with fruit flavour ice cream sauce.

Opposite

These ice cream dreams are a departure from traditional cupcakes, with chocolate-covered crispy rice cake as the base. You could make your own fruit purée or melt chocolate to drizzle over the top, then sprinkle with tiny sweets or chopped nuts.

Flowerpot

Materials:

Chocolate cupcakes, domed on top

Chocolate-covered stick biscuits or
   chocolate sticks

Small jelly sweets

White chocolate, melted

Tools:

Small piping bags

Non-stick baking paper

Instructions:

1 Pipe a small blob of melted white chocolate on to non-stick baking paper. Lay the end of a chocolate-covered stick biscuit or chocolate stick into the chocolate. Leave to cool and set (this can be speeded up by putting the stick and chocolate in the refrigerator).

2 When set, pipe another small blob of chocolate on top of the first one, and stick in coloured jelly sweets to form a flower. Attach a couple of green jelly sweets lower down the stick, using melted chocolate. Leave to cool and set.

3 Push the chocolate stick stem into the top of the cupcake.

Opposite

These potty cupcakes make a lovely alternative to a pot plant as a gift, or they will be a real hit at children's parties.

Wedding Cake

Materials:

Cupcakes baked in silver cases, flat-topped

Cupcakes baked in tiny silver sweet cases

Fondant icing (see page 14)

Sugar modelling paste/ flower paste

Small amount of green buttercream

Tools:

Small rolling pin

Small rose-petal cutter

Piping bags

Palette knife

Instructions:

1 To make an arum lily, roll out sugar modelling paste or flower paste thinly. Cut out small rose petals with the rose-petal cutter. Roll each one between your fingers to form a spiral with the point of the petal at the top. Leave to one side to set.

2 Spread warmed white fondant icing over each cake, placing the tiny cake on top of the larger one straight away so that it will stick.

3 Pipe small green stems and long leaves on the cakes and press the flowers into place.

These beautiful cakes could also be served for wedding anniversary celebrations, made in different coloured cases. As an alternative, make the cakes in gold cases, and colour the fondant icing to a soft ivory.

White Christmas

Materials:

Cupcakes

Fondant icing (see page 14)

White or green sugarpaste for the trees

Edible sparkles

Tools:

Sharp, pointed scissors

Piping bags

Palette knife

Instructions:

1 Make a solid, pointed cone shape from around 20g (¾oz) sugarpaste. Starting at the point of the cone, snip tiny 'v' shapes with sharp, pointed scissors, close to the surface of the paste, working round and down to look like a simple fir tree. Cut off the bottom of the cone when you get to the size of tree you would like.

2 Spread the top of each cake with warmed fondant. Stick the prepared tree on to the top of the cake while the fondant is still soft.

3 Sprinkle the tree and cake with edible sparkles.

Snow Drift

For another spectacular Christmas treat, bake the cake in a gold case and make the tree in white sugarpaste. Pipe a garland of fondant around the tree using a piping bag with the end cut off.

Ladybird

Materials:

Cupcakes with domed tops (carved to form a smooth dome)

Red sugarpaste

Black sugarpaste

Small piece of white sugarpaste for the eyes

Buttercream or jam for sticking the icing to the cake

Icing sugar for rolling out paste

Tools:

Small rolling pin

Palette knife

Small circle cutters

Instructions:

1 Make a circle template large enough to cover the whole of the dome of the cake. You might find a bowl or saucer in the kitchen to use as a template.

2 Spread a little buttercream or jam on each cupcake ready to stick on the sugarpaste.

3 Roll out the red sugarpaste and cut out using the circle template. Lay the paste on the cake and smooth it out evenly. Mark a line across the middle with the palette knife for the wings.

4 Roll out black sugarpaste, cut out a smaller circle, dampen it slightly with water and stick it on to the edge to the cake for the face. Cut off the excess to the edge of the red paste.

5 Use the edge of a small circle cutter to press in a smiling mouth.

6 Eyes and spots on the back can be cut out using small circle cutters, or moulded by hand. Make two small circles of white sugarpaste and stick on to the face. Make two smaller black circles, and stick them on top of the white. Two larger circles of black stuck on to the back make the ladybird's spots.

What a Buzz!

Cover the cake with a large circle of black sugarpaste. Make the face in the same way as the ladybird. Cut out strips of yellow sugarpaste and stick on to the black. Wings can be made by cutting oval shapes from rice paper. Make incisions in the paste where the wings will go, and push the ends of the wings in.

Family Tree

Materials:

Work out how many cupcakes you need for your family tree

Buttercream (see page 12)

Chocolate buttercream; add up to 30ml/ 2 tablespoons cocoa powder to buttercream until you get the shade you like

Skin-coloured sugarpaste: I used paprika food colouring, but different skin colours can be made by using different strengths or mixing shades of autumn leaf, paprika, chestnut and dark brown

Black food colouring for the eyes

Food colouring for hair, and green for leaves

Tools:

Palette knife

Piping bags

Piping tubes: plain no. 2 and leaf

Cocktail stick

Drinking straw – cut off the end at a slight angle for marking smiling mouths

Instructions:

1 Model skin-coloured sugarpaste into oval and round shapes for simple faces. Mark a smile on each with the end of a drinking straw.

2 Make tiny noses and stick them on. You could also make ears, if they are in character.

3 Spread chocolate buttercream on each of the cakes, and gently press the faces into place.

4 Mark the eyes by dipping the end of a cocktail stick into black food colouring, then pushing it into each face.

5 Pipe the name on each cake with buttercream.

6 Mix up small amounts of buttercream with food colouring for the hair and pipe the hair on for each character.

7 Mix buttercream with green food colouring. With a leaf tube in a piping bag, pipe green leaves over the rest of each cake.

This collection of cupcakes would be a lovely surprise for a family reunion, a grandparent's birthday, or to mark a new arrival in the family. Leaves could be made from sugarpaste cut out with different leaf cutters, rather than piping. Instead of a family tree, you could make named cakes for children coming to a birthday party.

Engagement Ring

Materials:

Cupcakes baked in gold cases

Extra gold cake cases for the lids

Fondant icing (see page 14)

Chocolate stick biscuits

Small amount of sugarpaste for the ring

Colourless firm jelly sweets

Edible sparkles

Gold powder food colouring

Alcohol for painting

Tools:

Palette knife

Sharp, pointed scissors

Instructions:

1 Spread each cake with warmed fondant icing. Push two chocolate stick biscuits into the cake to support the 'lid'.

2 Make a short thin sausage of sugarpaste and stick on the top of the cake to look like the ring. Make a slight dip in the middle to hold the 'diamond'. Paint with gold powder food colouring.

3 With sharp, pointed scissors, cut a colourless firm jelly sweet to a rough diamond shape. For added shine, roll the 'diamond' in edible sparkles. Stick it on to the ring by dampening slightly with water (not wet).

4 Put a small amount of warmed fondant in the empty cake case. When it has cooled and set (this should take only a few minutes) turn the case over and push the chocolate sticks gently into the fondant, to form the lid.

A tasty and romantic treat for an engagement party! Different coloured jelly sweets could be used to create a variety of precious stones.

Shamrock

Materials:

Cupcakes

Orange sugarpaste

Green sugarpaste

Small amount of buttercream or jam

Icing sugar

Tools:

Wavy-edged round cookie cutter,
    slightly bigger than your cake

Heart cutter

Palette knife

Rolling pin

Instructions:

1 Spread a little jam or buttercream on each cake.

2 Roll out the orange sugarpaste, with a little icing sugar to stop it sticking to the surface.

3 Cut out the sugarpaste with the large cutter and lay the icing over the cake. Smooth it with your hand.

4 Roll out the green sugarpaste and cut out three heart shapes for each shamrock. Lay them straight on to the cake as shown. If they need to be stuck on, dampen under each heart slightly with water.

5 Make a small green stem from the sugarpaste.

Sweet Thistle

Use purple sugarpaste for the top of the cake. Stick on a small flattened ball of purple sugarpaste and mark with a knife as shown. Roll out green sugarpaste and cut out two holly leaves with a cutter and the central shape by hand. Attach the central shape under the purple strands. Mark with 'v' shapes. Stick the two holly leaves underneath and mark the leaves with a knife.

Decorated Cookies

by Lisa Slatter

Cookies are easy to make, fun to decorate and great to eat. Whether you are a complete beginner or a sugarcraft enthusiast, you are sure to find something in this book to delight and inspire you.

Cookies make the perfect little gift and can be themed, decorated and personalised to suit any special occasion. If time is short it is possible to use shop-bought cookies for your projects. Choose firm shortbread-type bases for decorating. Gingerbread also works well. Lovely as they are, gooey, soft cookies are not suitable as they are too soft and will break.

Storage

Once cooled, the undecorated cookies can be stored in an airtight container for up to four weeks. Alternatively you can freeze them until ready for use. Make sure they are thoroughly defrosted before attempting to decorate them as any dampness or moisture will make the icing 'sweat' and the colours will run.

Decorated cookies will be at their best if consumed within two weeks of making. This will depend upon the recipe used. Package them in clear plastic party bags and tie with ribbon to secure. Do not keep decorated cookies in an airtight container as this will cause the icing to sweat, encourage mould growth and cause the colours to run.

Royal icing

Royal icing is used for piping detail on to the cookies. You can buy ready-to-mix packets in the supermarket, but it is just as quick and easy to make your own: lightly beat an egg white then slowly beat in 250g (9oz) of sifted icing sugar (confectioner's sugar). When the icing looks glossy and forms soft peaks it is ready to use.

Baking cookies

I have used this recipe to make all of the cookies in this book. It makes a firm and tasty cookie, which is simple to make and provides an ideal base for decorating.

The quantities given here are enough to make approximately fifteen medium-sized cookies.

Ingredients:

200g (7oz) caster sugar

200g (7oz) unsalted butter or margarine

1 medium egg

400g (14oz) plain all-purpose flour

Additional flour for kneading and rolling out

Preparation time: 8 minutes

Cooking time: 8 to 10 minutes, gas mark 4 (180°C/350°F)

Alternative flavours:

Chocolate cookies: replace 50g (2oz) plain flour with 50g (2oz) cocoa powder

Orange or lemon zesty cookies: add the zest of one orange or one lemon

Vanilla cookies: add the seeds from one vanilla pod or ½ teaspoon of good quality vanilla essence

Method:

1 Place the caster sugar and unsalted butter or margarine into a mixing bowl, together with any flavouring, and lightly cream together.

2 Crack one medium egg into a jug and lightly beat with a fork or small whisk.

3 Add the beaten egg to the creamed mixture together with all of the plain flour. Gently mix together. If you are using an electric mixer, set it to a slow speed and use the paddle attachment. The mixture will at first look like bread crumbs, which will eventually come together to form a dough.

4 Gather up the dough and, if necessary, knead by hand to incorporate all of the ingredients.

5 Place in a plastic bag, then into the fridge for at least two hours before use. This helps to stop the cookie dough from spreading during cooking. The cookie dough may be frozen if required. Defrost thoroughly before use.

Baking the cookies:

Cut-out method using cookie cutters

1 Pre-heat the oven to gas mark 4 (180°C/350°F). Lightly grease a baking sheet using spray oil.

2 Remove the cookie dough from the fridge and lightly knead. On a lightly floured surface, roll out the dough between a pair of marzipan spacers, to obtain an even depth.

3 Use cookie cutters to cut out the cookie shapes then place them carefully on to a greased baking sheet using a pallet knife. Cook equally sized cookies together to ensure even baking.

4 The cookies should be cooked for 8 to 10 minutes until they are a light golden brown. Remove from the oven and place on a wire rack to cool. The cookies will be soft and springy to the touch at this stage but will firm up as they cool down.

Using cookie treat pans and cookie sticks

Note: only use cookie sticks that state they can be placed in an oven and withstand high temperatures. Lollipop sticks are not suitable.

1 Lightly spray the cookie treat pan with some spray oil.

2 Take a piece of cookie dough and push it into the cookie treat pan until it fills up the shape to just below the top edge. If you wish to make cookies on sticks, place a stick on to the back of the dough and lightly push in place. Cover the back of the stick with a little more cookie dough and smooth into place. Cook in the same way as described for cut-out method.

3 Alternatively, cookie sticks can be inserted into the cookies as soon as they are removed from the oven while the dough is still soft and springy. This method can also be used for cookies made from cut-out shapes.

Equipment

To bake the cookies used in this book you will need scales for weighing out ingredients; an electric mixer with a paddle attachment; a spatula; a fork or small whisk; a jug; plastic bags; a baking sheet; spray oil; marzipan spacers; a large rolling pin; an angled pallet knife; a selection of cookie cutters, metal and plastic; 15cm (6in) and 20.5cm (8in) cookie sticks (suitable for going into an oven); cookie treat pans in various shapes; a wire cooling rack; and an airtight container.

All of the equipment you need to get started with your decorated cookies.

Making faces

Adding carefully modelled and painted facial details will bring your characters to life. Use these simple techniques to create great faces.

Mouth

1 Push the bottom edge of a round cutter into the sugarpaste and rock from side to side.

2 With a paintbrush and a little pink powdered food colouring, add a soft pink hue to the mouth by running the brush along the indentation.

Cheeks

Use a flat brush and some pink powdered food colouring in a circular motion to add colour to the cheeks.

Eyes

1 Push a ball tool into the sugarpaste to make a round indentation.

2 Wiggle the ball tool up and down to change the shape to an oval.

3 Fill the oval with a small ball of white sugarpaste and flatten into place.

4 Push the ball tool into the white sugarpaste to make an indentation.

5 Fill the indentation with a small ball of coloured sugarpaste.

6 Make a small indentation into the coloured area of sugarpaste.

7 Fill this with a tiny ball of black sugarpaste.

8 Paint a white highlight into the black of the eye with white powdered food colouring mixed to a paint with white alcohol.

9 Paint a fine black line around the top of the eye then paint eyelashes and eyebrows. Use black paste food colouring mixed with a little white alcohol.

Ears

1 Roll a small ball of sugarpaste.

2 Cut it in half.

3 Flatten and stick to the side of the head with water. Indent with a ball tool to hollow out a little and shape.

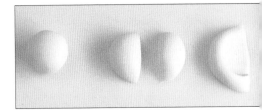

Nose

1 Push a ball tool into the sugarpaste to make a small indentation.

2 Roll a tiny ball of sugarpaste and stick it into the indentation with water.

3 Flatten slightly then push a veining tool into the underside twice to create the nostrils. Highlight with a little pink powdered food colouring.

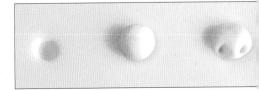

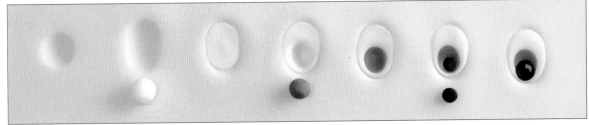

Ahoy There!

Ingredients:

Round-shaped cookies

Sugarpaste (or rolled fondant): dark brown, light brown, black, red, white, yellow

Paste food colouring: dark brown

Powdered food colouring: pink, white, gold

White alcohol (or lemon extract)

Icing sugar (or confectioner's sugar)

Equipment:

23cm (9in) rolling pin

Ball tool

Flower/leaf veining tool

Fine paintbrush

12mm (½in) flat paintbrush

25mm (1in) circle cutter

Small sharp knife

6mm (¼in) round pressure piping tube (ST17)

Instructions:

1 Dust the work surface with icing sugar and roll out some light brown sugarpaste. Flip it over and paint the back with water using the flat brush.

2 Cover the cookie with the sugarpaste, taking it right down over the edges. Smooth in place then trim off any excess at the back with a knife.

3 Cut a wide strip of red sugarpaste and stick it across the top of the head, smoothing over the edges. Trim off the excess then pull a veining tool diagonally across the surface to make three indentations.

4 Mark the positions of the facial features with a ball tool, making a small central indent for the nose and two larger ones above this on either side for the eyes.

5 Push the edge of a circle cutter into the sugarpaste underneath the nose to create the mouth. See page 55: 'Making faces'.

6 Roll a tiny ball of paste and stick it in place for the nose. Mark in the nostrils with a veining tool (see page 55).

7 Roll a ball of sugarpaste and cut in half for the ears. Flatten each half, stick to the side of the head then hollow and shape with a ball tool (see page 55).

8 Dust on some rosy cheeks and add a soft pink hue to the mouth with a paintbrush and some pink powdered food colouring.

9 Create the eye following the instructions on page 55.

10 Cut out a circle of black sugarpaste, trim a small strip from one edge to form the patch and stick it in place where the other eye should be. Ensure the straight edge is flush with the bottom edge of the hat.

11 For the hair, stick small flattened teardrops of dark brown sugarpaste at the sides of the head, around the ears, and texture with a veining tool.

12 Make two small cones out of red sugarpaste, flatten and stick to the edge of the hat, to one side. Stick a ball of red sugarpaste on top and mark with the veining tool so it looks like a knot.

13 For the earrings, roll two balls of yellow sugarpaste, flatten, and cut a hole in the centre of each one with the piping tube. Stick at the base of the ears with water then paint gold using gold powdered food colouring mixed with a little white alcohol.

14 Paint stubble with a fine brush and some dark brown paste food colouring mixed with some white alcohol.

Try changing the colours for a fairer skinned, blond version of the pirate.

Hubble and Bubble

Ingredients:

Cookies shaped like ice-cream cones

Sugarpaste (or rolled fondant): dark
  brown, green, white, black, yellow

Paste food colouring: black or
  dark brown

Powdered food colouring: pink, white

White alcohol (or lemon extract)

Icing sugar (or confectioner's sugar)

Equipment:

23cm (9in) rolling pin

Ball tool

Flower/leaf veining tool

Fine paintbrush

12mm (½in) flat paintbrush

Small sharp knife

Piping tube

25mm (1in) star cutter

10mm (½in) star plunger cutter

Ribbon cutter or mini cutting wheel

Instructions:

1 Dust the work surface with icing sugar and roll out some green sugarpaste. Flip it over and paint the back with water using the flat paintbrush.

2 Cover the cookie with the sugarpaste, taking it right down over the edges. Smooth in place then trim off any excess at the back with a knife.

3 Cut a wide strip of black sugarpaste, lay this over the top of the cookie and stick it in place to create the hat. Take the icing right down over the sides and trim as before.

4 Mark the positions of the facial features with a ball tool. Start in the centre with a small indent for the nose, then place two larger oval indents above this on either side for the eyes.

5 Push the wide end of a piping tube into the sugarpaste underneath the nose to create the mouth.

6 Create the eyes, nose and mouth following the instructions on page 55.

7 Make several flattened teardrop shapes from brown sugarpaste and stick them on either side of the head to create the top part of the bunches. Merge them together and add texture by pulling a veining tool repeatedly over the surface of the sugarpaste from top to bottom.

8 Stick a teardrop shape at the base of the hair on either side to make the lower part of the bunches. Texture as before.

9 Make the fringe from two small sausage shapes of brown sugarpaste. Lay these at the base of the hat and on top of the hair at each side. Add texture as before.

10 To create the brim of the hat, cut a medium-sized strip of black sugarpaste and stick across the base of the hat, just covering the edge of the hair. Cut a thin yellow strip with a ribbon cutter and stick this along the centre of the brim. Trim the excess with a sharp knife.

11 Cut out a small yellow star and stick a tiny black star in the centre of it. Stick this on to the front of the hat. Repeat this process, reversing the colours, to make two further stars. Attach these to the witch's bunches on either side of the face.

Use the same techniques, but change the colours to make a good witch or fairy godmother.

Rabbit, Rabbit

Ingredients:

Rabbit-shaped cookies

Sugarpaste (or rolled fondant):
  light brown, dark brown, white, pink, black

Paste food colouring: dark brown

Powdered food colouring: pink, white, brown

White alcohol (or lemon extract)

Icing sugar (or confectioner's sugar)

Equipment:

23cm (9in) rolling pin

Ball tool

Flower/leaf veining tool

Fine paintbrush

12mm (½in) flat paintbrush

Small sharp knife

Instructions:

1 Dust the work surface with icing sugar and roll out some light brown sugarpaste. Flip it over and paint the back with water using the flat paintbrush.

2 Cover the cookie with the sugarpaste, taking it right down over the edges. Smooth in place then trim off any excess at the back with a knife.

3 Mark the positions of the facial features with a ball tool. Start in the centre with a small indent for the nose and place two larger oval indents above this on either side for the eyes.

4 Rub a ball tool into the middle of each of the ears to make long oval indentations. Roll small sausages of pink sugarpaste, stick one into each indentation, then flatten and smooth them into place with your fingers.

5 Roll a marble-sized ball of light brown sugarpaste and cut it in half. Roll each half into a cone shape. Stick each one horizontally, with the point innermost, on to the cookie, just below the nose indentation.

6 Flatten them slightly then repeatedly drag a veining tool over the surface from the inner point out towards the outer edge of the shape, to create the fur effect.

7 Use the veining tool to add a few more textured lines to the chin area, around the sides of the cookie, around the bottom of the ears and above the nose. Dust over the textured areas with brown and white powdered food colouring.

8 Stick a tiny teardrop of white sugarpaste in the middle underneath the textured cheek area. Flatten then divide in half with a veining tool to make the teeth.

9 Softly dust the cheeks and the middle of the ears with a little pink powdered food colouring.

10 Make a small cone of brown sugarpaste; insert it point downwards into the indentation made for the nose. Flatten slightly then indent at the bottom on either side for the nostrils. Paint with a little dark brown paste food colouring mixed with white alcohol.

11 Make the eyes following the instructions on page 55.

*Prepare the white rabbit in the
same way, just change the colour
of the icing to white and, when
painting the eyes, paint long
eyelashes for a girl.*

Winter Cheer

Ingredients:

Snowman-shaped cookies

Sugarpaste (or rolled fondant): white, light blue, black, brown, green, red, orange

Paste food colouring: black

Powdered food colouring: white, pink

White alcohol (or lemon extract)

Icing sugar (or confectioner's sugar)

Edible lustre spray: pearl

Edible white glitter dust

Equipment:

23cm (9in) rolling pin

Ball tool

Flower/leaf veining tool

Fine paintbrush

Small sharp knife

12mm (½in) flat paintbrush

25mm (1in) circle cutter

Small triple holly leaf plunger cutter

6mm (¼in) round pressure piping tube (ST17)

Instructions:

1 Roll out the white sugarpaste. Cover the cookie with the sugarpaste, taking it right down over the edges. Smooth in place then trim off any excess at the back with a knife.

2 Make indentations under the arms with a veining tool. Spray all over with pearl lustre spray.

3 Push a ball tool into the front of the body three times to position the buttons. Roll three small balls of black sugarpaste, stick these into the indentations and flatten slightly.

4 Cut a wide strip of brown sugarpaste. Stick it across the top of the head and over the sides to form the hat. Smooth it into place. Trim off the excess with a knife.

5 Pull a veining tool over the top of the hat to make a couple of creases, and horizontally across the hat just up from the base to create the brim.

6 Cut out a green triple holly leaf and stick it on the brim of the hat.

Add three tiny red balls of sugarpaste for the berries.

7 Cut three thin strips of blue sugarpaste. Stick one around the neck, trimming off the excess at the sides to create the scarf. Mark a fringe with a veining tool at the bottom of the other two strips, then trim and stick these in place. Use a veining tool to mark the edge of the knot and add texture to the scarf.

8 Mark indentations for the nose and eyes.

9 Push a circle cutter into the sugarpaste below the nose to make the mouth. Mark the two scoops on either side with the piping tube.

10 Dust the cheeks and the mouth with some pink powdered food colouring.

11 Fill each eye socket with a small ball of black sugarpaste and flatten.

12 Paint a highlight into each eye with white powdered food colouring and black eyebrows with paste food colouring, both mixed to a paint with white alcohol.

13 Make the carrot nose from a cone of orange sugarpaste. Roll a veining tool over the surface to texture and stick on to the face.

14 Mix white edible glitter dust with white alcohol and paint on to the scarf and on to the top and brim of the hat.

Change the colour scheme and add ear muffs. Roll a ball of lilac sugarpaste, cut it in half and stick it to the sides of the head. Snip into the icing repeatedly with scissors to create the bobbly effect.

Jingle Bells

Ingredients:

Bell-shaped cookies

Sugarpaste (or rolled fondant): white

Edible lustre spray: pearl and gold

Icing sugar (or confectioner's sugar)

Confectioner's glaze

Equipment:

23cm (9in) rolling pin

Bell-shaped cookie cutter (the same size
    as you used to make the cookies)

Ribbon cutter or mini cutting wheel

Embossing mat

Fine paintbrush

12mm (½in) flat paintbrush

Small sharp knife

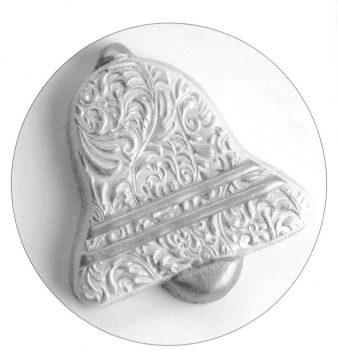

Instructions:

1 Dust the work surface with icing sugar and roll out some white sugarpaste to an approximate depth of 3mm (⅛in). Dust the surface with a little icing sugar.

2 Lay an embossing mat on top of the sugarpaste and roll over this with a small rolling pin so as to emboss the design on to the surface. Carefully lift off the embossing mat.

3 Cut out a bell shape from the sugarpaste using the bell-shaped cookie cutter.

4 Flip the sugarpaste cut-out over and paint the back with a little cooled boiled water using the flat paintbrush.

5 Place the sugarpaste cut-out on to the cookie and gently pat into place so as not to flatten the embossing.

6 Spray the cookie all over with some pearl edible lustre spray.

7 Use the gold lustre spray as a paint to add detail. Spray it on to a plate and use a fine paintbrush to brush the colour on to the raised embossed pattern on the surface of the bell.

8 With a ribbon cutter or mini cutting wheel, cut out two thin strips of sugarpaste and stick them across the base of the bell with a little water, leaving a small gap in between them. Trim to fit with a small sharp knife.

9 Paint the top of the bell, the clanger and the strips with gold lustre spray.

10 To set the colour and add shine, paint the gold areas with a little confectioner's glaze.

Make an alternative design suitable for a wedding or birth celebration by covering the cookie with a smooth sugarpaste cut-out bell and decorating with small cut-out daisies. Emboss the centres of the daisies with a daisy embossing stick and spray the whole cookie with pearl lustre spray. Paint on gold detail as before.

Baby Face

Ingredients:

Round-shaped cookies

Sugarpaste (or rolled fondant): light brown, peach, black, pink

Paste food colouring: dark brown

Powdered food colouring: pink, white

White alcohol (or lemon extract)

Icing sugar (or confectioner's sugar)

Equipment:

23cm (9in) rolling pin

Ball tool

Flower/leaf veining tool

Fine paintbrush

12mm (½in) flat paintbrush

Round cutters, 45mm (1¾in) and 25mm (1in) diameter

Small sharp knife

6mm (¼in) round pressure piping tube (ST17)

Instructions:

1 Dust the work surface with icing sugar and roll out some peach sugarpaste. Flip over and paint the back with water using a flat paintbrush.

2 Cover the cookie with the sugarpaste, taking it right down over the edges. Smooth in place then trim off any excess at the back with a knife.

3 Mark the positions of the facial features with a ball tool, starting in the centre with a small indent for the nose and then placing two larger indents above this on either side for the eyes.

4 Push a 45mm (1¾in) round cutter into the sugarpaste underneath the nose to create the mouth. Mark the scoops at either side of the mouth with a 6mm (¼in) piping tube.

5 Roll a tiny ball of sugarpaste and stick it in place for the nose. Mark in the nostrils with a veining tool (see page 55).

6 Roll a ball of sugarpaste and cut it in half for the ears. Flatten each half and stick one on each side of the head. Push a ball tool into the centre of each to form a hollow and shape (see page 55).

7 Add some rosy cheeks at the edge of the mouth, using the flat paintbrush and some pink powdered food colouring. Draw the same brush along the mouth area to give it a soft pink hue.

8 Roll two small balls of black sugarpaste and stick them into the eye sockets. Pat and smooth into place with your finger.

9 Paint a highlight into each eye with white powdered food colouring mixed with a little white alcohol. Paint the eyelashes and eyebrows in place with dark brown paste food colouring.

10 For the hair, roll three thin sausage shapes of light brown sugarpaste, twist each one into a curl and stick to the top of the head with water.

11 For the bow, cut out a 25mm (1in) circle of pink sugarpaste and cut it in half to form two semi-circles. Fold each semi-circle in half and stick together at the ends with water. Secure to the head on top of the hair with a little water.

12 Place a ball of pink sugarpaste in the centre of the bow. Flatten and add detail with a veining tool.

For the baby boy, secure the bow with water under the chin to make a bow tie.

Magical Butterfly

Ingredients:

Butterfly-shaped cookies

Sugarpaste (or rolled fondant): dusky pink, burgundy, orange

Icing sugar (or confectioner's sugar)

White alcohol (or lemon extract)

Powdered food colouring: gold

Sugar balls: pink

Equipment:

23cm (9in) rolling pin

Butterfly-shaped cookie cutter

Fine paintbrush

12mm (½in) flat paintbrush

Single rose petal cutter: large

Cone/serrated cone tool

Flower/leaf veining tool

Fancy leaf cutter

Ball tool

Instructions:

1 Dust the work surface with icing sugar and roll out some dusky pink sugarpaste. Cut out the butterfly shape using the cookie cutter.

2 Paint the back of the butterfly cut-out with a little water using the flat brush and stick it on to the cookie. Gently smooth it into place, paying particular attention to the edges of the sugarpaste, rubbing these with your fingers to create a curved, smooth appearance.

3 Pull a veining tool into the icing at the sides of the butterfly in between the top and bottom wings, and also down through the centre of the butterfly to make an indentation. Roll a sausage of orange sugarpaste for the body and stick over the indentation with a little water.

4 Paint the body with a little water, then push a line of pink sugar balls into the orange icing. Paint the tops of the sugar balls with a little gold powdered food colouring mixed with white alcohol.

5 Roll out some burgundy sugarpaste quite thinly. Cut out two fancy leaf shapes and stick these centrally on to the bottom pair of wings. Pull a central vein down the middle of each one using a veining tool. Paint the vein gold.

6 Cut out two large burgundy single rose petals and stick these in the centre of the top pair of wings with a little water. Pull a veining tool up through the middle and again on either side to create three indentations on the surface of the icing. Paint with gold.

7 Push a ball tool into the end of the fancy leaf shapes and at the end of each vein on the rose petal shape. Roll tiny balls of orange sugarpaste and stick these into the indentations. Now, push the serrated cone tool into the centre of each one to create a star effect. Paint them all with gold.

8 Using a fine paintbrush, paint a gold edge around the edge of the butterfly. Paint additional detail on to the surface of the butterfly with gold powdered food colouring mixed with white alcohol.

A very different look can be
created by simply swapping
the colours around, using the
burgundy as the base colour
with dusky pink cut-outs.

Christmas Holly

Ingredients:

Holly-shaped cookies

Sugarpaste (or rolled fondant):
   dark green, red

Confectioner's glaze

Icing sugar (or confectioner's sugar)

Equipment:

23cm (9in) rolling pin

Holly-shaped cookie cutter

Flower/leaf veining tool

Ball tool

Fine paintbrush

12mm (½in) flat paintbrush

Instructions:

1 Shake a little icing sugar on to your work surface and roll out some dark green sugarpaste to an approximate depth of 3mm (⅛in). Cut out a holly shape using the holly-shaped cookie cutter.

2 Flip the sugarpaste cut-out over and paint the back with a little cooled boiled water using the flat paintbrush.

3 Place the sugarpaste cut-out on to the cookie. Gently smooth into place, paying particular attention to the edges of the sugarpaste, rubbing these with your fingers to create a curved and smooth appearance.

4 Using the sharp end of the veining tool, pull a central vein down the centre of the holly leaf.

5 Repeat the process, pulling shorter lines out from the central vein towards the outer edge on each side.

6 Push a ball tool into the icing at the base of the leaf to make three small indentations for the berries to sit in.

7 Roll three small balls of red sugarpaste and stick them into the indentations at the base of the leaf using a little cooled boiled water.

8 Paint the leaves and berries with some confectioner's glaze to add a high gloss finish.

Opposite

Use an embossing mat to add texture to the surface of the leaves. Roll out some white sugarpaste to an approximate depth of 3mm (⅛in) and dust the surface with a little icing sugar. Lay an embossing mat on top of the sugarpaste and roll over it with a small rolling pin so as to emboss the design on to the surface of the icing. Cut out the holly shape then repeat steps 4 to 8 above. Spray the cookie with some gold and then some pearl edible lustre spray. Lustre spray can also be used as a paint to add detail. Spray on to a plate and use a paintbrush to brush the colour on to the holly berries and the surface of the leaf. Glaze with confectioner's glaze.

Fairy Castle

Ingredients:

Cookies shaped like wedding cakes

Sugarpaste (or rolled fondant): white, green, pink

Edible lustre spray: pearl

Powdered food colouring: silver

White alcohol (or lemon extract)

Icing sugar (or confectioner's sugar)

Royal icing: white

Sugar balls: silver

Equipment:

23cm (9in) rolling pin

Wedding cake cookie cutter

Swirl-textured rolling pin

Straight frill zig-zag cutter

Small blossom plunger cutter

Mini cutting wheel

25mm (1in) circle cutter

Serrated cone tool

Flower/leaf veining tool

12mm (½in) flat paintbrush

Piping bag

1.5mm round or writing tube (ST2)

Ruler

Instructions:

1 Shake a little icing sugar on to your work surface and roll out some white sugarpaste. Texture with a swirl-textured rolling pin. Cut out the wedding-cake shape with the cookie cutter.

2 Paint the back of the cut-out with water using the flat paintbrush, stick it on to the cookie then spray with edible pearl lustre spray.

3 Cut the turrets out of sugarpaste using the zig-zag side of a straight frill cutter. Trim the width of the zig-zag strip to approximately 1cm (½in). Stick to the top edge of the cookie with water and trim off the excess flush with the sides. Repeat for the other two layers of the cake.

4 Mark and remove a 3cm (1¼in) section from the middle of the bottom turret to make room for the door.

5 Using a mini cutting wheel, cut the door from a piece of sugarpaste. First cut an oblong measuring 5 x 3cm (2 x 1¼in), then round off the top corners to make an arch shape. Stick in place with water.

6 Mix silver powdered food colouring with white alcohol and paint it on to the turrets and door.

7 Push a silver ball into the sugarpaste at the base of each turret along the top and bottom layers of the cake.

8 Push a serrated cone tool into the gaps in between the silver balls. Do the same along the length of the middle turrets, around the top of the door arch and along the bottom edge of the door.

9 Mark the outer window on the door using a 25mm (1in) circle cutter and the inner circle with the wide end of the piping tube. Pull a veining tool across the inner window in one direction and then the other to make a trellis pattern.

10 Flatten a tiny ball of sugarpaste and stick it to the door to make a door handle. Mark four indents into the handle with a veining tool.

11 Using a small blossom plunger cutter, cut pink blossoms from swirl-textured sugarpaste.

12 Make leaves by flattening small cones of green sugarpaste, veining the centre and pinching the wide end together.

13 Place a 1.5mm piping tube into a piping bag, fill with royal icing and use this to stick the flowers and leaves in place around the door. Stick silver balls into the centres of the flowers with a little royal icing.

For a different look, cover the cookie with ivory-coloured sugarpaste, spray with gold lustre spray and use gold-coloured sugar balls to replace the silver ones. Make the window in the door slightly smaller and omit the trellis work. Finish with dark peach flowers.

Summer Sunflowers

Ingredients:

Sunflower or daisy-shaped cookies

Sugarpaste (or rolled fondant): red, brown

Edible lustre spray: gold, bronze

Icing sugar (or confectioner's sugar)

Equipment:

23cm (9in) rolling pin

Sunflower or daisy-shaped cookie cutter

Flower/leaf veining tool

12mm (½in) flat paintbrush

Mini basketweave rolling pin

Round/wavy-edged cutter, 35mm (1¼in) round side/40mm (1½in) wavy side

Lily petal cutters, 5cm (2in) and 4cm (1½in) length tip to tip

Instructions:

1 Shake a little icing sugar on to your work surface and roll out some red sugarpaste. Cut out the flower shape with the cookie cutter.

2 Paint the back of the cut-out with a little water using the flat paintbrush and stick it on to the cookie.

3 Rub the edges of the sugarpaste to create a curved and smooth appearance.

4 Vein the centre of each petal with a veining tool, pulling it up through the middle of each petal and radiating outwards a few times.

5 Cut out five individual petals using the large lily cutter. Vein as before and stick the petals on to the cookie with a little water. Position these petals so that they alternate between every other petal on the first layer.

6 Repeat the process for the next layer, this time using the smaller lily-petal cutter, placing these in between the petals in the previous layer. Vein as before.

7 Push the 35mm (1¼in) round cutter into the centre of the sugarpaste on the cookie. Cut out and remove the circle of sugarpaste.

8 Roll out some brown sugarpaste to an approximate depth of 3mm (⅛in). Texture with a mini basketweave rolling pin then cut out a 40mm (1½in) wavy-edged circle.

9 Paint the back of the circle with water and stick it into the centre of the flower.

10 Pull a veining tool repeatedly over the outer edge of the wavy-edged circle to texture it and blend it to the base of the petals at the centre of the flower.

11 Spray some bronze and gold lustre spray on to a plate and use the flat paintbrush to brush some bronze and gold highlights on to the petals and the centre of the flower.

Change the colour scheme of the flower by using a golden yellow sugarpaste for the petals instead of red.

3-2-1 Blast Off!

Ingredients:

Cookies shaped like space rockets

Sugarpaste (or rolled fondant): blue, green, yellow, orange, red

Icing sugar (or confectioner's sugar)

Equipment:

23cm (9in) rolling pin

Space rocket cookie cutter

Ribbon cutter or mini cutting wheel

Round/wavy edged cutters, 25mm (1in) round side/40mm (1½in) wavy side

Large star plunger cutters

12mm (½in) flat paintbrush

Flower/leaf veining tool

Cone/serrated cone tool

Instructions:

1 Shake a little icing sugar on to your work surface and roll out some blue sugarpaste. Cut out the rocket shape using the rocket cookie cutter. Cut a small strip away from the nose of the rocket and the tail of the rocket.

2 Flip the sugarpaste cut-out over and paint the back with a little cooled boiled water using the flat paintbrush.

3 Place the sugarpaste cut-out on to the cookie. Gently smooth into place, rubbing the edges of the sugarpaste with your fingers to create a curved and smooth appearance.

4 Mark lines on the edges of the wings with a veining tool.

5 Roughly mix some yellow and orange sugarpaste together so that it becomes marbled in appearance. Cut out the tail of the rocket with the cookie cutter. Trim to size and stick it to the tail of the rocket. Mark straight lines all the way across with the veining tool.

6 Roll out some green sugarpaste. Cut out the nose of the rocket using the cookie cutter. Trim to size and stick to the top of the cookie. Mark straight lines all the way across with the veining tool.

7 Cut out three yellow stars and stick them evenly spaced across the tail of the rocket. Push a serrated cone tool into the centre of each one to emboss a small star shape.

8 Cut three thin strips of green sugarpaste with a ribbon cutter or mini cutting wheel. Stick one at the base of the nose, one just below the wings, and the other near the tail (refer to the picture). Mark each strip all the way across with a serrated cone tool.

9 Cut out a 40mm (1½in) wavy-edged circle in yellow sugarpaste, a smaller plain 25mm (1in) circle in red and a yellow star. Stick the red circle on top of the yellow wavy-edged one and stick the yellow star in the centre of the red circle. Push a serrated cone tool all around the edge of both circles and into the centre of the star.

Reverse the colour scheme making the rocket green with blue accents. Insert silver balls into the indents made by the serrated cone tool for an alternative look.

Loveable Teddies

Ingredients:

Cookies shaped like teddy bears

Sugarpaste (or rolled fondant): light brown, ivory, black, white

Paste food colouring: black

Powdered food colouring: brown, white, pink

Edible glitter dust: white

White alcohol (or lemon extract)

Sugar balls: pink

Icing sugar (or confectioner's sugar)

Equipment:

23cm (9in) rolling pin

Teddy bear cookie cutter

Mini quilting wheel

Flower/leaf veining tool

Ball tool

Fine paintbrush

12mm (½in) flat paintbrush

4cm (1½in) five-petal blossom cutter

Round/wavy-edged cutters, 25, 35, 5mm (1, 1¼, 1¾in) round side/40mm (1½in) wavy side

Small sharp knife

Instructions:

1 Shake a little icing sugar on to your work surface and roll out some light brown sugarpaste. Cut out the teddy bear shape using the cookie cutter. Flip over and paint the back with water using a flat paintbrush.

2 Cover the cookie with the sugarpaste, taking it right down over the edges. Smooth in place then trim off any excess at the back with a knife.

3 Pull a veining tool up under the arms, and around the neck and ears to indent the icing.

4 With a ball tool, indent the centre of the ears, then rub the ball tool from side to side on the ends of each of the paws to make oval indentations.

5 Run the mini quilting wheel down the centre of the teddy, then all around the outside edge.

6 Fill each ear with a small ball of ivory-coloured sugarpaste and smooth into position with your fingers. Fill each paw with a sausage of ivory-coloured sugarpaste and smooth it into place.

7 Cut a 45mm (1¾in) circle of ivory sugarpaste and stick it on to the tummy. Then cut a 4cm (1½in) blossom from light brown sugarpaste and stick it to the centre of the circle. Stick three pink sugar balls into the flower's centre with water.

8 Edge the ears, paws, tummy circle and blossom with a stitching line using the mini quilting wheel. Mix white edible glitter with white alcohol and brush it into the ears, and on to the paws and flower centre.

9 Cut out a 35mm (1¼in) circle of light brown sugarpaste and stick it to the centre of the bear's head to form its snout. Smooth down the outer edges with your finger, leaving it raised in the centre.

10 Mark an indentation for the nose and two for the eyes.

11 Take a 25mm (1in) circle cutter and push the bottom edge into the sugarpaste to make a smiley mouth. Link the nose and mouth with a straight embossed line.

12 With a flat brush, dust the cheeks and the mouth with some pink powdered food colour. Also dust around the sides of the bear and over his snout with a little brown powdered food colour.

13 Fill each eye socket with a small ball of white sugarpaste and flatten. Make a small indentation with a ball tool in each eye, fill with a small ball of black or dark brown sugarpaste and flatten.

14 Paint a white highlight into each eye using powdered food colour mixed with a little white alcohol, and paint eyelashes with black paste food colour mixed with white alcohol.

Replace the flower with a light brown sugarpaste wavy-edged circle cut-out. Push a single white sugar ball into the centre of it. Paint eyebrows instead of eyelashes.

Home Sweet Home

Ingredients:

Cookies shaped like cupcakes

Sugarpaste (or rolled fondant): pale yellow, dark blue, light blue, orange

Powdered food colour: gold

White alcohol (or lemon extract)

Icing sugar (or confectioner's sugar)

Royal icing: green

Equipment:

23cm (9in) rolling pin

Cupcake cookie cutter

Mini cutting wheel

Flower/leaf veining tool

12mm (½in) flat paintbrush

Fine paintbrush

Ribbed rolling pin

Ruler

Piping bag

Small (2mm) leaf tube (ST50)

6mm (¼in) round pressure piping tube (ST17)

Small serrated closed scallop crimper

Medium-sized blossom plunger cutter

Small sharp knife

Instructions:

1 Shake a little icing sugar on to your work surface and roll out some pale yellow sugarpaste. Texture with a ribbed rolling pin, then cut out the cup-cake shape ensuring that the ribbing runs vertically.

2 Paint the back of the cut-out with water using the flat paintbrush, then stick it on to the cookie.

3 Cut a wide strip of dark blue sugarpaste and stick this to the top half of the cookie to create the roof, taking the icing right down over the edges of the cookie. Trim off the excess with a sharp knife.

4 Cut a 1.5 x 2cm (½ x ¾in) chimney from dark blue sugarpaste using a ruler. Stick it to the roof.

5 Crimp across the bottom edge of the roof and the top part of the chimney with the small serrated closed scallop crimper. Paint the crimped edge with gold powdered food colour mixed with a little white alcohol.

6 Cut small circles of pale yellow sugarpaste with a 6mm (¼in) round piping tube and stick them on to the roof.

7 Cut two 1.5cm (½in) squares of dark blue sugarpaste for the windows and stick them in place. Mark a windowsill across the base of each one with a veining tool and make a pattern on the windows with the end of the veining tool. Paint the windowsills gold (see step 5).

8 Cut an oblong door measuring 2.5 x 3.5cm (1 x 1½in) with a mini cutting wheel from dark blue sugarpaste. Round off the top corners to make an arch. Mark a 1cm (½in) square window with a veining tool and texture as for the windows. Place a flattened ball of sugarpaste on the side of the door for a handle and mark with a veining tool. Stick the door to the cookie and paint the window and door handle with some gold powdered food colour mixed with white alcohol.

9 Pipe some green royal icing leaves with a small leaf piping tube at the base of the cookie under the windows.

10 Cut out some light blue blossom flowers using the blossom plunger cutter and stick them on to the leaves. Place a ball of orange sugarpaste in the centre of each flower and push a veining tool into the centre four times to make the button centres.

Make a red house in exactly the same way, but change the colour scheme to burgundy, cream and dark peach.

Christmas Spirit

Ingredients:

Star-shaped cookies in four different sizes

Sugarpaste (or rolled fondant): green

Edible lustre spray: pearl

Icing sugar (or confectioner's sugar)

Royal icing: white

Sugar balls: white

Equipment:

23cm (9in) rolling pin

Stacking star cookie cutters: 9.5, 8, 7 and 5cm (3¾, 3¼, 2¾ and 2in)

Marzipan spacers

12mm (½in) flat paintbrush

25mm (1in) circle cutter

Small sharp knife

Piping bag

1.5mm round or writing tube (ST2)

Swirl-textured rolling pin or texture mat

Scissors

Instructions:

1 Shake a little icing sugar on to your work surface and roll out some green sugarpaste. Texture with a swirl rolling pin or texture mat. Cut out four different-sized stars.

2 Paint the back of the star cut-outs with a little water using a flat paintbrush and stick them on to the cookies.

3 Roll some green sugarpaste between marzipan spacers to give an even depth, then use a 25mm (1in) circle cutter to cut out three thick circles of sugarpaste. Allow to dry. These will act as spacers in between the cookies.

4 With a little royal icing, stick the dried sugarpaste circles into the centres of the three largest iced stars.

5 Stack the four stars on top of one another, alternating the points of the stars as you go, securing each one in place with a little royal icing.

6 Make a long, tapered cone of green sugarpaste, ensuring the base of the cone fits comfortably in the middle of the smallest star.

7 Roll out a little more green sugarpaste and texture it with the swirl rolling pin. Flip the paste over and moisten the back with a little water.

8 Lay the prepared cone on to the textured sugarpaste and carefully wrap it around the cone. Press the two raw edges of sugarpaste together close to the side of the cone to join them securely. Cut away any excess with a pair of scissors. Smooth the join a little with your fingers.

9 With a sharp knife, cut the base of the textured cone flat then stick to the centre of the smallest star with a little royal icing.

10 Place a 1.5mm piping tube into a piping bag and fill with white royal icing. Pipe a little royal icing on to the points of the stars and stick a white sugar ball at each point. Stick a few more around the sides of the cone and one on top.

11 Spray the whole cookie with a little pearl lustre spray.

Use white sugarpaste, textured with a circles embossing mat. Add pink sugar balls for a trendy alternative.

A Touch of Romance

Ingredients:

Heart-shaped cookies on cookie sticks

Sugarpaste (or rolled fondant): white, peach, dusky pink

Icing sugar (or confectioner's sugar)

Edible lustre spray: pearl

Sugar balls: white

Equipment:

23cm (9in) rolling pin

12mm (½in) flat paintbrush

Flower/leaf veining tool

Small blossom plunger cutter

Fine paintbrush

Six-petal flower eyelet cutter

Heart cutter, 8.5cm (3¼in) top to bottom

Small sharp knife

Ball tool

Instructions:

1 Shake a little icing sugar on to your work surface and roll a ball of peach-coloured sugarpaste. Cut it in half and stick each half on to the cookie, just down from the top, to create the bust area.

2 Roll out some more peach-coloured sugarpaste, paint the back with water and cover the cookie, taking it right down over the edges. Smooth in place then trim off any excess at the back with a knife.

3 Roll out some dusky pink sugarpaste. Texture the surface by lightly pressing a six-petal flower eyelet cutter all over the surface. Cut out an 8.5cm (3¼in) heart shape, flip it over and paint the back with water using the flat brush.

4 Stick the heart shape on to the cookie so that the top of the heart covers the bust. Smooth the sugarpaste into place around the sides of the cookie, cutting off any excess with a small sharp knife.

5 Mark a couple of indentations under the bust on either side with a veining tool.

6 Cut out a small blossom flower from white sugarpaste using a blossom plunger cutter and stick it in the centre of the bodice on the top edge. Push a ball tool into the centre of the flower, then stick a small ball of pink sugarpaste into the hollow this makes. Push a veining tool into the centre four times to create a button effect.

7 Lightly spray the bodice with pearl edible lustre spray. Also spray some lustre spray on to a plate and use it as a paint for the fine detail on the bodice, highlighting the centres of the embossed flowers.

8 Paint a ring of water around the neck area. Push some white sugar balls on to this to create a necklace. Paint the surface of the white balls with some pearl edible lustre spray to make them look like pearls.

Packaged in clear party bags and tied with ribbon, these cookies make lovely wedding favours.

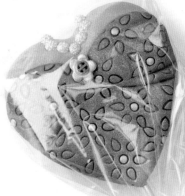

Change the colour of the icing to dark blue. This time add straps to the bodice by sticking white balls over the shoulders. Paint these with some pearl edible lustre spray.

Clowning Around

Ingredients:

Round-shaped cookies

Sugarpaste (or rolled fondant): red, white, yellow, green, black

Paste food colour: black

Powdered food colour: pink

White alcohol (or lemon extract)

Icing sugar (or confectioner's sugar)

Confectioner's glaze

Royal icing

Instructions:

1 Shake a little icing sugar on to your work surface and roll out some white sugarpaste. Paint the back with a little water using the flat brush. Cover the cookie with the sugarpaste, taking it right down over the edges. Smooth in place then trim off any excess at the back with a sharp knife.

2 Cut a wide strip of green sugarpaste and stick it across the top of the head, smoothing over the edges. Trim off the excess with a sharp knife.

3 Cut out some small yellow stars and stick them all over the hat.

4 With a ball tool, make an indentation for the nose to sit in. For the nose, roll some red sugarpaste into a ball and stick it into position. Glaze with confectioner's glaze.

5 For each eye, mark a cross into the icing with a veining tool. Fill the cross indentation with a thin sausage of

Equipment:

23cm (9in) rolling pin

Ball tool

Flower/leaf veining tool

Fine paintbrush

12mm (½in) flat paintbrush

Small star cutter

Small sharp knife

Half-moon cutter

Piping bag

1.5mm round or writing tube (ST2)

black sugarpaste and smooth into place. Using a fine paintbrush, paint a wiggly eyebrow above each eye with some black paste food colour mixed with white alcohol.

6 For the mouth cut a half-moon shape out of red sugarpaste using a half-moon cutter and stick it in place. Lay a thin white sausage on top of this in the centre, flatten and pull into shape with a ball tool, then mark a dividing line through the centre with a veining tool.

7 For the hair, stick small flattened teardrops of yellow sugarpaste at the sides of the head, and blend and texture with a veining tool.

8 Roll a sausage of green sugarpaste, flatten slightly then stick to the bottom of the hat to form the brim. Trim off the excess at the sides with a sharp knife.

9 Roll another green sausage of sugarpaste, flatten it then concertina it to make the ruff. Cut a straight edge to one side. Fill a piping bag with a writing tube (ST2) and some royal icing. Use this to stick the ruff around the bottom of the face. Cut a thin yellow strip of sugarpaste and stick this on top of the ruff. Mark it into sections with a veining tool then make an indent in the centre of each section with a ball tool.

10 Add a soft pink hue to the cheeks with a flat paintbrush and some pink powdered food colour.

Change the colour scheme to black and white, add a daisy to the hat with a sugar-button centre and change the shape of the eyes, adding a small bell-shaped piece of sugarpaste over the eyes for the eyelids.

Sweet Baby

Ingredients:

Cookies shaped like romper suits

Sugarpaste (or rolled fondant): light blue, white

Icing sugar (or confectioner's sugar)

Royal icing: black

Equipment:

23cm (9in) rolling pin

Mini quilting wheel

Flower/leaf veining tool

12mm (½in) flat paintbrush

Small teddy bear cutter

Small sharp knife

Ribbon cutter or mini cutting wheel

Piping bag

1mm round or writing tube (ST1.5)

Ball tool

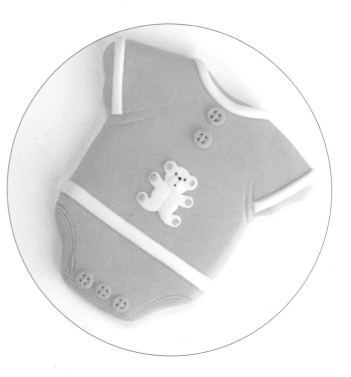

Instructions:

1 Shake a little icing sugar on to your work surface and roll out some light blue sugarpaste. Flip it over and paint the back with water using the flat brush.

2 Cover the cookie with the sugarpaste, taking it right down over the edges. Smooth in place then trim off any excess at the back with a knife.

3 Pull a veining tool up under the arms a couple of times to indent the sugarpaste.

4 Roll out some white sugarpaste and cut out four equal-sized strips using a ribbon cutter.

5 Stick these with water to the cookie around the neck and arms, and just below the waist. Trim to fit with a knife. Run a mini quilting wheel along the edge of each strip on both sides to create a stitch line.

6 Create a double stitch line along the bottom edge of the romper suit and around the legs.

7 Make five buttons from tiny flattened balls of blue sugarpaste. Stick two to the cookie just below the neck, and the remaining three at the base of the cookie between the legs. Push a veining tool into the centre of each button four times to create a button effect.

8 Roll out some white sugarpaste fairly thinly. Cut out a small teddy bear shape and stick it to the centre of the romper suit. Run the mini quilting wheel through the centre of the teddy from top to bottom.

9 For the snout add a small flattened oval of sugarpaste to the face and make an indent with a ball tool centre top for the nose.

10 Push a ball tool into the paws and into the ears. Fill each one with a tiny ball of blue sugarpaste, smoothing into place with a ball tool.

11 Pipe the eyes, nose and mouth with a little black royal icing using a writing tube, size ST1.5.

Change the colour of the icing to pale pink.
Stick a flower to the centre and use a mini
quilting wheel to make stitch lines down the
centre of each petal. Finish with a sugar button
in the centre of the flower.

Rose Bouquet

Ingredients:

Oval/egg-shaped cookies

Sugarpaste (or rolled fondant): brown, yellow, green

Edible lustre spray: gold

Icing sugar (or confectioner's sugar)

Confectioner's glaze

Royal icing: green

Modelling paste: yellow, green, white

Equipment:

23cm (9in) rolling pin

Mini basketweave rolling pin

Small- and medium-sized rose leaf plunger cutters

Number cutters

12mm (½in) flat paintbrush

Small sharp knife

Piping bag

1.5mm round or writing tube (ST2)

Ball tool and balling pad

Instructions:

1 Shake a little icing sugar on to your work surface and roll out some brown sugarpaste. Roll a mini basketweave rolling pin over the surface to create a basketweave texture. Flip the sugarpaste over and paint the back with water using the flat brush.

2 Cover the cookie with the sugarpaste, taking it right down over the edges. Carefully pat in place so as not to destroy the embossing. Trim off any excess at the back with a knife.

3 Roll a thin sausage of brown sugarpaste and, with a little water, secure it around the edge of the top half of the cookie to make the handle.

4 Roll another thin sausage of brown sugarpaste, fold it in half and twist the two pieces together to create a rope effect. Stick this horizontally across the centre of the cookie to create the rim of the basket.

5 Using two sizes of rose-leaf plunger cutters, cut out and vein several leaves from green modelling paste. Place on to a balling pad and rub a ball tool around the edge of the leaf to soften and shape. Stick these on to the top half of the basket, just under the handle coming down to the rim.

6 Make several ribbon roses. For each one roll a sausage of yellow modelling paste, and pinch along the top edge to thin the icing down. With the thin edge uppermost, roll one end inwards to make a cone, then continue to roll the rest of the icing around the cone, squashing the base in as you roll. To finish, turn the end back on itself, pinch underneath and cut away any excess paste with a sharp knife. Fill a piping bag with a writing tube (ST2) and some green royal icing. Use this to stick the roses in place.

7 Spray some gold edible lustre spray on to a plate and with a flat brush add some gold highlights to the basket, leaves and roses.

8 Roll out some white modelling paste quite thinly. Cut out a number 50 (or whichever number you like) and spray with gold lustre spray. Stick to the front of the basket with a little water. Paint over with confectioner's glaze.

Use red roses and cut out a suitable message or word from red sugarpaste with some alphabet cutters and stick it on to the basket. Mix red edible glitter with white alcohol and paint over the letters and edges of the roses to give the cookie some sparkle.

Marry Me!

Ingredients:

Cookies shaped like wedding cakes

Sugarpaste (or rolled fondant): ivory

Edible lustre spray: pearl

Powdered food colour: pink, green

Icing sugar (or confectioner's sugar)

Royal icing: white, green

Ready-made five-petal royal-iced
    flowers: yellow

Edible white glitter dust

Equipment:

23cm (9in) rolling pin

Wedding cake cookie cutter

12mm (½in) flat paintbrush

Flower/leaf veining tool

Small serrated closed scallop crimper

Piping bags

Small (2mm) leaf tube (ST50)

1.5mm round or writing tube (ST2)

Instructions:

1 Shake a little icing sugar on to your work surface and roll out some ivory sugarpaste. Cut out the wedding-cake shape with the cookie cutter.

2 Paint the back of the cut-out with a little water using the flat brush and stick it on to the cookie.

3 Rub the edges of the sugarpaste to create a curved and smooth appearance.

4 Pull a horizontal dividing line across the cookie between each cake layer using a veining tool.

5 Use a small serrated closed scallop crimper to crimp a border at the bottom of the cake. Dip the ends of the crimper into some icing sugar then gently push the crimper into the sugarpaste. Squeeze the crimper ends together while they are inserted into the icing, slowly release the squeeze and then pull the crimper out from the icing. Repeat the process until the whole bottom edge has been crimped.

6 Use the crimper in the same way to create the side design on each tier. Crimp diagonally across each tier, then crimp a shorter line just above and just below the first line to complete the design.

7 Spray the whole cookie with edible pearl lustre spray.

8 Dust the edges of the yellow ready-made flowers with a little pink powdered food colour.

9 Place the writing tube (ST2) into a piping bag and fill with a little white royal icing. Pipe a little royal icing on to the surface of the cookie and stick the flowers in place: one flower on the top tier, three on the second tier and three on the bottom tier.

10 Place the small leaf tube (ST50) into a piping bag and fill it with a little green royal icing. Pipe leaves into the gaps around the flowers. Once dry, dust with a little darker green powdered food colour to enhance.

11 Sprinkle some white edible glitter all over the surface of the cookie.

Cover the cookie with white sugarpaste and use white flowers with a dusted pink edge to change the look.

Lucky Ducks

Ingredients:

Duck-shaped cookies

Sugarpaste (or rolled fondant): white, brown

Paste food colour: black, orange

Powdered food colour: white, yellow, light brown

White alcohol (or lemon extract)

Icing sugar (or confectioner's sugar)

Confectioner's glaze

Equipment:

23cm (9in) rolling pin

Duck-shaped cookie cutter

Ball tool

Flower/leaf veining tool

Fine paintbrush

12mm (½in) flat paintbrush

Instructions:

1 Shake a little icing sugar on to your work surface. Roll out some white sugarpaste. Cut out the duck shape with the cookie cutter.

2 Paint the back of the cut-out with a little water using the flat brush and stick it on to the cookie.

3 Rub the edges of the sugarpaste to create a curved and smooth appearance.

4 Push a ball tool into the centre of the head to mark the position for the eye.

5 Roll a small ball of brown sugarpaste and stick it in place for the eye. Flatten it with your finger.

6 With a veining tool pull a line across the centre of the duck's beak dividing it in two. Make a small indent at the back of the beak on the top half, and then draw in the back of the beak.

7 Starting at the head and working down towards the tail, drag the veining tool over the body to create the feather effect.

8 Make a wing from a flattened cone of white sugarpaste. Stick the wing on to the side of the body with a little water and texture it in the same way as the body.

9 Mix some yellow powdered food colour with some white alcohol and paint the duck all over using the fine brush. Once dry, add additional colour to the head, back, tail and wing by dusting with light brown powdered food colour.

10 Mix a little orange paste food colour with some white alcohol. Paint the beak.

11 With a fine paintbrush and some black paste food colour, paint a circle of black into the eye. Add a highlight to the eye with white powdered food colour mixed with white alcohol.

12 Add a high gloss finish to the beak and the eye by painting them with some confectioner's glaze.

Change the colour scheme of the duck by painting a cream base instead of a yellow base and dust with dark brown powdered food colour instead of light brown.

Publishers' note

If you would like more information about sugarcraft, try the following:

Sugar Animals by Frances McNaughton, Search Press, 2009

Sugar Fairies by Frances McNaughton, Search Press, 2010

Sugar Flowers by Lisa Slatter, Search Press, 2010